The Ladybug Who Lived On A Four Leaf Clover

Written by Emily Franke

Illustrated by Haley Franke

Emily Franke ♡

The Ladybug Who Lived On A Four Leaf Clover

©2022 Emily Franke
Illustrated by Haley Franke

Published by AcuteByDesign

Library of Congress Number
2022936197

ISBN Number
978-1-943515-52-3

ACUTE BY DESIGN
the little book company that could

In loving memory of Sheila Q. Franke
June 10, 1938 - June 26, 2021

My twin sister, Haley and I
are dedicating this book to honor our
beautiful, beloved grandmother.

She was always a kind woman that
strove for love, peace, and unity.

We love you, Grandma!

Once upon a time there was a beautiful ladybug
who lived on a four leaf clover.
Her name was Sheila.

Sheila lived in the backyard of a little girl named Emily.

Sheila would smile while flying around the sky,
landing on those who needed a reminder of hope.

She was a very special ladybug who brought lots of love, kindness and good luck to everyone who found her.

Emily was always a bright and happy young girl.
One day, she lost someone very special to her; her grandmother.
Emily's parents told her that her grandmother had gone to heaven.

Emily was very sad. She missed her grandmother
and wished she could see her and hug her one more time.

The next day, while walking in her backyard, Emily stumbled upon a bright red and black polka dot ladybug sitting on a four leaf clover.

 8 Emily smiled and was reminded of the times when she and her grandmother would search for four leaf clovers in the grass.

Emily picked up the four leaf clover and immediately
felt the presence of her grandmother around her.

Suddenly, Emily felt the sun shining brightly on her face.
She could hear the beautiful singing of the birds
and then heard something else.

She heard a sweet voice whispering in the wind that said,
"Hello my dear, Emmy!"

"Grandma! Is that you?" Emily shouted.

The ladybug opened her magical wings and
flew onto Emily's hand.

"Yes Emmy." The ladybug said.

"It is me. I will always be with you. I'm forever in your heart."

Emily twisted her fingers around the four leaf clover and wept,
"But Grandma, I miss you. How will I know you're with me?"

The ladybug always knew what to say.
With her wisdom, she looked at the sweet girl and said,

"My dear Emmy, whenever you are feeling sad, take yourself back to when we used to look for four leaf clovers in the grass."

18

Emily smiled and felt at peace.

19

She closed her eyes and made a wish on the four leaf clover.

22 Emily was so excited! She ran into the house to tell her family.

"Mom! Dad! Guess what?" said Emily.

23

Both of her parents ran towards the back door
and couldn't believe what they saw.

They saw Emily holding a ladybug on a four leaf clover.

25

Emily hugged her parents and said, "I'm not sad anymore.
I know grandma is always with me."

After that special day, Emily always told the story
about the ladybug who lived on a four leaf clover.
She hoped that it would help fill others with happiness and love and
bring good luck to all.

27

There are signs everywhere, just look around!

In loving memory of Sheila.

Made in the USA
Middletown, DE
07 May 2022

65467030R00022